Superhero Status
A Superhero Guide to Leadership

Dr. Ashley B. Hosey

Be the Hero!

Lead!

[signature]

Dedication

This book is dedicated to all the Superheroes who have saved me, inspired me, helped me, trained me and fought alongside me

Introduction
Not Every Superhero Can Fly

We encounter a variety of people daily. Every so often we meet someone that is different or special, and they stand out as unique. They have extraordinary gifts, talents, and skills. They also accomplish great tasks, achieve big goals, and reach huge levels of success. These feats leave passersby, relatives, and acquaintances in amazement about how these individuals do such things. Truly they are not ordinary or average. They are more than merely human. In fact, they must be superhuman. That's it! They're superheroes.

In our world when problems and difficult times arise, there are people who handle ordinary problems. Yet, when major problems occur, the superheroes take over. A superhero is someone special with extraordinary abilities. This superhuman constantly performs feats of excellence that are marveled and admired by all. Superheroes are the ones that not only save the day but on occasion, they save the world, too!

Even outside the pages of comic books and off the screens of blockbuster movies, superheroes are real. Do they have real superpowers? Can they fly? Can they shoot lasers from their eyes? Do they swing from tall buildings? Of course, not. The superhero's superpowers or super abilities are simply their gifts and talents. Whether they are born with them or acquire them by other means, superpowers can range from the outwardly obvious to more subtle manifestations.

These individuals exist in our daily lives and in our workplaces and organizations. We cross paths with them regularly; however, we often fail to recognize them for who they really are. Nevertheless, the definition of a superhero is simple. Regardless of their powers, costumes, and abilities, superheroes in both the fiction world and the real world are known and recognized by two distinguishing traits. First, they can recognize when people in their community, city, or world stand in need of help. Secondly, they consistently use their gifts to make a difference.

"My heroes have the heart to live the life I want to live."

Gnarls Barkley, *Crazy*

1

Who Are the Superheroes?

When the fate of the world has hung in the balance, there have been a select few to step from the shadows and save the day. These select few show leadership in times of confusion and panic. They often take doubt and defeat and turn them into certainty and definite victory. Many others find inspiration and motivation through their actions. These individuals rally others together and instill confidence to the masses. They are called by many different names, but without a doubt, they are superheroes.

The superhero is an individual who possesses great skill, talents, and abilities, and uses their gifts positively to help others. They are the leaders we strive to be. Moreover, they are people of action who assume many roles. Superheroes appear wherever there is a need or a job to be done. They lead by doing, and they get the job done regardless of the circumstances. A good superhero is often the stuff legends are made of and the person stories are told about for generations.

What is the secret that makes a superhero a legend? It is not the talents or powers they possess. Neither is it the uniform they wear or the gadgets they use. It is their leadership style. Superheroes are the ultimate leaders. Anyone who wants to save the world must be willing to lead and sacrifice by example. Understand that the superhero's style of leadership is not for everybody. While it may look easy, it is not. Therefore, not everybody can or will be a superhero. These unique people do things other people can't or won't do, and they make it look easy. Only a select few who have the talent and fortitude will rise to the level of superhero leadership status.

Whether in the real or fiction world, superheroes often exhibit good examples of leadership styles that are employed through special gifts or powers. How those superpowers are used is most important. The secrets of superhero leadership are revealed in the pages of this book. As you read further, you will find all the information needed to identify superheroes, to understand superhero leaders, and to release the superhero leader within yourself. The purpose of this book is to share with you the time-honored secrets of superhero leadership. You will learn how these leaders respond to a challenge, how they train, and how they think. You will also learn how to identify superhero leadership qualities in yourself and others. Most importantly, you will gain insight on how to use the knowledge and wisdom that superhero leaders possess.

Superheroes are special people who appear at special times. Within the pages of this manual is the key to all the information you will need to start your path to learn the superhero leadership method and achieve superhero status. This information has been collected from the study and practice of many superheroes. For a clearer understanding as you read this book, substitute the word "leader" for "superhero" and substitute "talent or skill" for "superpowers." After reading, you will be able to positively answer the questions in the Superhero Survey at the end of the book.

The Superhero Profiles

"Know thyself."
Socrates

2

Superhero Profiles:
What Type of Superhero are you?

The world of the superheroes is very diverse and immense. Superhero leaders can range in abilities, powers, and personalities. Each one is unique; however, there are some general profiles of their personality styles which can be used to classify and identify them. These classifications help to make sense of the superhero universe that is ever-expanding. Some heroes may be in multiple categories or fit multiple profiles depending on their moods, the situation, their experiences, and the time or point in their career. The superhero profiles are generalizations based on the superhero's style, how they get the job done, their personality, or how they may use their superpowers. These profiles should only be used as a foundation since there are many new and emerging styles every day!

3

The Spotlight Superhero

This superhero has the highest visible profile of any superhero. He or she is very popular in the workplace. Popularity fuels the legend and stories of this type of hero. Even his enemies are in awe of him, which sometimes can fuel the enemies. The spotlight superhero's popularity may be further enhanced by a charming personality, good looks, marketing appeal, witty personality, public speaking skills, killer smile, or other engaging personal skills. Everyone wants to be this superhero.

They earned their popularity by performing their complex tasks or completing a difficult mission which may have been high profile or highly publicized. During these actions, the person displayed an extraordinary amount of talent while many people watched or the word of what they accomplished spread like wildfire. They continue to maintain their status by continually performing at a high level, and most of their battles and victories are high profile and in the view of the public. Therefore, this superhero is always in a huge public spotlight, in demand, and popular.

Everyone relies heavily on this type of leader for big things, small things, and almost everything because they know that no matter what, this superhero will get it done. Everybody believes in this person, and they are very confident in the leader's abilities. Not only will the leader get it done, but he will usually do so with ease and in a very cheerful, upbeat manner. People come to rely on this hero far too much because they are always there and never let anyone down. This superhero is usually the first person called on, and some people believe that if they can't get it done, no one can. As far as the people are concerned, they can't be defeated. This superhero can bring everyone together and can unite the masses.

Even other superheroes love working with this leader. They sometimes even have their own fan clubs! However, as nice as this type of superhero sounds, there are some drawbacks and pitfalls as well. A spotlight superhero is at high risk of burn out. There is a lot of pressure being in the spotlight all the time. Everyone wants to shine with this leader. Many people make requests, solicitations, and demands of the spotlight hero. Everyone wants their attention on tasks both big and small, even if they can do it themselves. People can become so dependent on this superhero that they may not try as hard because they know they can rely on this person to always fly in and save the day. Eventually, every superhero gets tired because it is impossible to be everywhere and doing everything for everyone. The spotlight superhero can wear down and approach exhaustion faster than other types because the spotlight never goes down.

In addition, being in the public spotlight and being popular can create envy and jealousy towards the superhero, which breeds enemies and villains. There are many people who just want to see this leader fail because they hate their success and popularity. There are also the up and coming superheroes who want to be the next spotlight superhero. Those are the ones who are constantly plotting on how to get their chance in the spotlight, even if it means the downfall of the current leader! Inadvertently, because the spotlight superhero deals with high profile issues and problems, sometimes smaller or lesser problems can be overlooked, delayed, or forgotten. This can build some resentment, especially if you were the person affected by the smaller problems.

The focus on the spotlight superhero can be unforgiving. When this person makes a mistake, which eventually happens, people are even more disappointed because the expectations of this hero are extremely high. This can be very stressful because of the amount of pressure they can put on themselves to always get things right and to take care of everything. Furthermore, everything the superhero says or does in the spotlight is under scrutiny and criticized because everyone is watching. This pressure can not only be very difficult, it can also interfere with that superhero's mission. However, some can handle the additional stress and attention, and they make good spotlight superheroes.

4

The Shadow Superhero

This leader is not always considered a superhero because they shun the spotlight. They prefer to operate in the shadows away from the crowds and the glory. He or she often does the things that other people won't do or can't do. These tasks usually aren't "spotlight" worthy. However, being in the shadows behind the scenes allows this superhero to get more work done. In fact, this person is the workhorse of superheroes. Don't get me wrong... All superheroes work hard, but a shadow superhero outworks all other superheroes! Their superpower may be the ability to carry huge workloads. This is the superhero who works alone (solo career), has a few partners (collaborators), a few mentees (sidekicks), and is part of several different superhero leagues (alliances), teams, and organizations. This is all while being active in their local community, nationally, and even globally! He or she even has a long and varied gallery of villains. This is the superhero who works while everyone else sleeps and outworks everyone when they are awake.

The shadow superhero is almost the opposite of the spotlight hero in many ways. In some situations, this superhero may lack the luster, personality, glow, or charm of the spotlight superhero. The shadow superhero may not have the natural gifts or powers of the spotlight superhero. Nevertheless, he or she is often just as effective and sometimes an even better leader than the spotlight superhero... just without parades or fanfare.

The shadow superhero can do the job no one else is willing to do, and they're able to accomplish more because they are solely dedicated to their mission. The way he or she completes the mission may not be the flashy, popular, or traditional way that other people may be accustomed to seeing. Still, the job is always done and done well. Completing the mission regardless of the circumstances, obstacles, or if it seems impossible is the trademark of this superhero. This superhero typically shuns the spotlight, recognition, or accolades altogether, which sometimes adds to their unpopularity. For a shadow superhero, accomplishing their mission and doing the necessary work is all that matters. Anything other than the mission is a distraction and therefore unnecessary.

By working in the shadows, the shadow superhero can concentrate on the roots of the problem at hand. While most superheroes wait for problems to come to light and appear, a shadow superhero is constantly finding small problems and solving them before they burst into large problems or issues. A shadow superhero is often a preventive and proactive problem solver. This leader is constantly creating new strategies, creating game plans, developing training scenarios, reviewing trends, analyzing data, and evaluating the results. This superhero takes his work very seriously and gives it his all every time. They are the type of superhero who is always overly prepared for every scenario, has worked out all of the variables in the plans of action, and has reevaluated the last battle plan for errors and weak points.

The shadow superhero is very dedicated. This trailblazer possesses tremendous focus and determination because they strongly believe in their mission. A shadow superhero does not take breaks (as if superheroes even get breaks). He or she pushes to be the best and makes others better in the process.

This is the superhero you want on your team because of their work ethic. They may not have the strongest power, but their work ethic and habits compensate. Although the shadow superhero may often prefer to work alone most of the times (because other people sometimes slow them down), on occasion they will work with a partner or join teams to accomplish bigger or difficult missions.

Shadow superheroes quietly build great networks of partnership, collaboration, and support with other superheroes because they know that they will need help with the more difficult tasks. Because this person is clear on their mission, they can often help other superheroes find ways to accomplish it. This person also raises the skill, power levels, and confidence of other team members. However, when a shadow superhero works with another superhero or team, they often fade to the back and allow the other heroes to take the credit. For this superhero, there is no time for press conferences or spotlights because they have work to do and a mission to complete.

5

The Emotional Superhero

Every superhero holds some power in deep reserve which only surfaces in times of extreme emotion or distress. There are some superheroes who ride the waves of emotions to achieve their mission. When a situation becomes chaotic and everyone else starts to panic and worry, an emotional superhero arises. This type of leader can be one of the most powerful superheroes. While tapping into their emotions, they can grow in statue, power, abilities, and influence. They can push past physical and mental limitations to accomplish huge tasks and overcome insurmountable odds. The emotional superhero also can stir and rally the emotions within others. They can create an army of people to charge into battle and rally around their cause or issue. This superhero can also rally and energize other superheroes and bring back teams from the brink of defeat. This makes the emotional superhero a force to be reckoned with and a formidable opponent.

A calm and passive superhero in most situations, the emotional superhero's power and strength lives deep within. We all have a range of emotions we experience, which can be triggered as we live our daily lives. Life events can cause sadness, a sense of loss, anger, frustration, and stress. An emotional superhero's strength draws and grows based on the emotions they are experiencing. They can take these emotions that may hurt or debilitate other people and turn them instead into fuel for their power.

This leader is best in situations that seem hopeless, chaotic, unjust, and stressful. They work best when everyone else has given up and the outcome appears grim and impossible. The emotional superhero only accesses his or her great power when they are emotionally stirred up, there is a crisis or emergency, or there is a clear enemy that must be vanquished. Once their power is released, it usually is strong, limitless, and powerful because of the intense emotion and urgency at hand.

The emotion trigger for this superhero does not come from within the superhero, but most often comes from the people and situations around them. If the superhero is engaged in battle and focused on the mission, emergency, or the source of the irritation, their power is engaged. Once the mission is achieved and the focus is gone, so is their power. Emotional superhero powers like emotions quick, intense, and brief. Nonetheless, relying on emotions to trigger your gifts is not an efficient and reliable way to be a superhero. Yet, if the superhero can understand their superpower and access their emotion, they can control their power and use it at their will. To accomplish this, an emotional superhero will require lots of additional training to understand and use their power at full potential.

Emotional superheroes can turn the tide of battle and can rally the troops together, but they can disappear when the battle is complete. When accomplishing a mission, there are times for emotion, and there is also time for strategy, consistency, and subtlety. An emotional superhero can be lulled to sleep by removing their emotional trigger. If there's no stress, discord, or pressure present, there is no emotional superhero.

6

The Amazing Superhero

The amazing superhero is as described in their title. They perform feats that are awesome and perplexing at the same time. When they save the day, people often say things like: "How did they come up with that solution? Never in a million years would I have thought to do that!" This superhero is creative in their approach and problem-solving skills. The amazing superhero creates solutions to problems that no one could imagine. They solve problems with out of the box ideas and suggestions. For this leader, there is no box or limit, only answers that have not been created yet. They are gifted with great imaginations. They can make connections with parts of concepts, bits of ideas, parts of plans, and create new and outstanding ideas. They solve complex problems in simple ways. This superhero appears to create solutions and pull answers out of thin air! Amazing.

The amazing superhero takes losing situations and turns them into victories by applying dogmatic will and determination to see their ideas complete. In the end, people are left amazed and wondering how in the world they completed that mission, solved that problem or came up with that solution. When this individual comes up with a solution, they believe in the solution and can see its application when no one else can. Through force of will and heart, he or she can push through difficult circumstances, difficult obstacles, and difficult situations to victory. Not only is this type of leader gifted with creativity, they also have tremendous heart. They hold no hidden agenda. They hold no hidden ambitions. They believe so strongly in their mission and in their calling that their passion fuels them and drives them. They will always find a way to make it happen.

The amazing superhero is sometimes difficult to understand and difficult to follow. Other people and other superheroes cannot see the ideas that this person proposes, especially in the beginning. This makes some people wary of this superhero or doubt them because they cannot follow the hero's pattern of thinking or match their optimism. Others will tell this superhero that their idea will not work, and they will come up with ways to convince them to change directions. However, the success record of this leader builds and bestows confidence.

An amazing superhero can inspire others with their passion and heart even if others do not understand the problem, the solution, or how they operate. Time after time, they deliver. They fix the unfixable, and they solve every problem in a way the leaves people simply amazed at the outcome. No one can figure out how they did it, what they were thinking when they did it, why they did it, or how it occurred to them to do it! After an amazing superhero has saved the day, people worry less about how they did it and are simply glad they saved the day!

7

The Reluctant Superhero

Not every superhero is eager to use their abilities. As hard as that is to believe, there are truly some gifted individuals who do not want the burden of being a superhero. They either lack the confidence to be a superhero, or they have not accepted that they are superheroes. This leader does his or her best to hide their gifts. The reluctant superhero simply tries to blend in. They often do not have flashy or outwardly visible signs that may indicate super abilities. Their superpowers go unnoticed unless you are paying close attention to their leadership traits. The reluctant superhero has mastered avoiding drawing attention to themselves. Instead, this leader has learned to hide their powers to evade making others feel inadequate or to incur the jealousy or wrath that comes along with being a superhero.

They do not want to be a spotlight superhero or anything close to it. In fact, they may see being a superhero as a burden they are not ready or willing to take on. They have saved the day on occasion when the situation has called for it (and no other superhero answered the call). Then, they quickly went on with their daily lives. Most of the time this superhero will never be recognized or seen by others as a superhero. Only those people close around them may recognize their ability or power. Tasks just seem to magically get done when they are around. Missions just happen to get completed.

The reluctant superheroes have their reasons for not wanting to be known as a superhero. These leaders are often shy about their powers and abilities. They lack confidence in displaying their gifts, and especially in receiving recognition for them. Moreover, not all superheroes have good experiences the first time they use their abilities. People sometimes react with jealousy, envy, and other negative emotions. Other times, friends ostracize or disassociate with the person because they are gifted or have been able to do something great. In addition, once a superhero is identified, people begin to ask them for favors, they are sent on missions, they go into a battle, or they are given additional responsibilities. This can seem overwhelming, especially without some guidance or mentoring. Unfortunately, reluctant superheroes may have experienced a crushing or embarrassing defeat the first time they tried to be a superhero. Therefore, they choose to stay hidden, and they are reluctant to show their super abilities.

Despite their reluctance to show their gifts, this does not diminish their powers and abilities. These superheroes can contain an enormous amount of power and surprising ability… sometimes multiple superpowers. Nevertheless, because the reluctant superhero shies away from using their abilities, they may not know the depth and potential of their powers. They may not know how to use their powers properly or to their maximum. For this leader to become a full-fledged superhero, he or she may need additional training and mentoring. Most importantly, they need convincing.

8
The Legend Superhero

Just as a superhero is extraordinary compared to mere mortals, there is one superhero who leaves everyone in awe. This superhero's status exceeds any other superhero around them and places them in a league of their own. They are legend superheroes. They have mentored countless sidekicks, lead many alliances, participated on several successful teams, maintained a superb solo career, and accomplished numerous missions. They have fought mighty battles, achieved massive victories, and saved the world more times than can be counted. The legend superhero is the leader that everybody wants to work with and fight alongside.

Other superheroes tell stories about the times that they were saved by this superhero, when they were mentored by this superhero, or when they had the privilege of watching this superhero in action. When the legend superhero shows up, everyone's mind is set at ease and their confidence goes up. People count it a privilege to be saved by this superhero, and superheroes consider it a badge of honor to work with the legend superhero. Even in such a glorious career, this leader has met and made many villains. However, he or she has fought and won so many battles and campaigns that even villains do not want to face them.

In fact, deep down, villains even respect this superhero. Villains tell stories of being beaten by this superhero, watching this superhero beat every scheme and trap, and even how powerful this superhero was in action. Because of their earned respect, a legend superhero can negotiate ceasefires, de-escalate tensions, and bring waring or feuding parties to the negotiation table simply on the merit of their name alone. This superhero has evolved to the power level of having the superpower of universal respect.

The legend superhero commands the respect of everyone. Their record is unchallenged. Their abilities are admired by all. This superhero inspires all that they encounter. They take the time to encourage younger superheroes and sidekicks. They are available as resources of knowledge and strategy when needed. They teach other superheroes simply by sharing stories of their mission, victories, and battles. They are the superhero we all aspire to be. The legend superhero invests in other superheroes and in making others better superheroes. They join other superheroes in their missions, even when they are not needed. They also willingly let other superheroes take the lead and back their call to encourage superhero growth. When a superhero needs help, this is the person they seek out. When they do this, the legend superhero listens.

This leader is the superhero you want to please and not to disappoint. You want to honor them and make them proud of you. Even if you fail, the legend superhero will make you feel good while giving you support to get better and to do better. He or she encourages other superheroes to grow and surpass them in power and skill. They are advocates for all superheroes and are ambassadors of superhero goodwill. They serve in local missions, global missions, and even intergalactic missions because their reputation is that profound.

This superhero is a living legend. He or she is a superhero among superheroes who operate far above the skill level that most superheroes will never achieve. They never lose touch with their purpose or mission. The legend superheroes are the best and set the measure of expectation for all superheroes to follow. Only a legend inspires other legends.

Superhero Power Profiles

"Hide not your talents, they for use were made. What's a sundial in the shade?"
Ben Franklin

9

Superhero Powers

What would a superhero be without a superpower or the special ability which separates them from mere mortals? This ability defines them and categorizes them. A superhero's superpower is their basic talent and skill. It guides and determines how they interact with situations, scenarios, and other heroes. Moreover, it also determines how other people view them. Talent and superpowers can be numerous and very diverse. Every talent is unique to that superhero and can be used differently by every superhero. Every superhero has different skill levels for using his or her power depending on their training, experience, natural ability, and battle exposure.

Superheroes are not necessarily limited to one ability. Some heroes can have multiple talents or powers in various combinations. On a rare occasion, you can encounter a "top-level" superhero who seems to possess them all. Basic superhero talents can be generalized into the categories described in the upcoming chapters. If you can readily identify a superhero power or talent, it is easier to know how to interact, chose a team, or know which battles you may need help with or which situations you can be the most effective.

10

Super Strength

The most basic of all superpowers is super strength. It's the ability to be stronger than the average person. For most superheroes, this is one of their first abilities to be acquired, manifested, or discovered. Super strength is also recognized by a superhero's ability to lift and carry heavy loads, move immovable objects, push through barriers, knock down walls, and endure harsh environments and circumstances. Basically, a super strong hero can move the objects, lift the objects, endure longer, or carry the loads that other people may feel are impossible. This often leaves regular people amazed and in awe of how they can do that. It is also a power that inspires other people to reach their potential as well because strength resides in everyone and everyone can get stronger.

A super strong hero can run through the standing opposition, bust through walls, carry other comrades and people on their shoulders, and battle longer and farther. They are harder to be restrained or contained by the enemy. Not only can these superheroes pack a lot of power in a punch, but they can also carry huge workloads and weights on their shoulders. Furthermore, they can move immense objects and ones that appear to be immovable. Super strength also translates to super endurance or the ability to endure harsh conditions and attacks.

Strength levels can vary greatly depending on the superhero. While some superheroes can literally move mountains, others may only move a few boulders. The more battles and adventures a superhero engages in, the stronger they can become. A more experienced superhero's strength level will be higher than a less experienced hero. On the rare occasion that it is not, the experienced hero will still be stronger in most cases because they have acquired the wisdom on how and when to apply their super strength. They also understand that the wrong application of super strength can be a mistake and lead to disaster!

When assembling a team for a mission, it is very important to have strong superheroes on the team. Although the skill levels may vary and individually their strength level may not be high, together and collectively their overall strength level rises. Surrounding yourself with superheroes stronger than you will make you raise your strength level and potential. You do not have to be the strongest superhero on the team. In fact, no matter how strong you are, there is always someone a little stronger.

"Strength does not come from physical capacity. It comes from an indomitable will."

Mahatma Gandhi

11
Super Hearing

Super hearing is the ability to hear things better and clearer than the average person. It doesn't matter if the sounds are far away, at different frequencies, or slightly out of the range of normal hearing. A superhero with the power of super hearing can glean important information from conversations and filter out background noises, interference, and other static and focus on what is important. A super hearing superhero can hear things that other people simply cannot because super hearing is super listening. It is almost impossible to surprise a hero who has this ability because this leader does not miss any details.

A good super hearing superhero can often decipher if someone is telling the truth, their sincerity, or if they are omitting information because of their super listening. The ability to hear and listen allows this person to understand problems, issues, and possible underlying causes which may not be apparent to people not blessed with incredible hearing. This advantage also allows them to plan appropriately to solve problems, plan for problems, or clarify the proper strategies needed in a situation. Because hearing leads to understanding, a superhero with super hearing has a greater chance of doing the right thing and applying the correct tactics before making a mistake.

Super hearers can reveal and foresee the hidden and true nature of a person because they concentrate on what that person is saying instead of what they are actually doing. This allows superheroes with this gift to also predict with higher probability the future actions and motives of someone. They often appear to hear things that are not there. This is only because no one else can hear them yet. They can solve mysteries, conflicts, and negotiate sound strategies, often without applying any other superpower. Never underestimate the power of super listening.

12
Super Vision

Super vision is the ability to see things that other people cannot see or are not willing to see. This is the ability to see objects far away from a distance. It's the ability to see through objects, past objects and people, and the ability to see small, seemingly microscopic and finite details. Super vision is also the ability to see in the dark, in very low light, or in foggy unclear conditions. It is also the ability to see objects that move at very high rates of speed, when things change quickly, or when they become more complicated. There are many variations on the ability of super vision, but simply, it is the ability to see beyond the current situation.

A superhero with super vision can see things before they come into view of normal people. This can be helpful when setting a course, a heading, a direction, or avoiding trouble or traps. A leader with this ability can see through objects that block normal vision to see what is hidden behind or inside despite the outer appearance. Super vision can also give a superhero the ability to see details in an object or situation that are not obvious to other people. When normal people are blinded by fog, smoke, or covered in darkness, super vision allows you to see more clearly. This allows a leader to focus on their mission without straying from their chosen path or missing important items. This is extremely important when on team missions and leading a team through difficult terrain and circumstances.

It is always good to have a superhero on your team with super vision. Moreover, it is extremely important that your team leader has this talent. A team leader with this gift can keep his team from getting lost or separated but most importantly assure that their team reaches their goal. This power, when combined with super hearing, can become an extraordinary sensory perception power (see Chapter 14 ESP).

13
Super Speed

Super speed is the ability to move a high rate of speed. It is not limited to covering distances in a shorter period. In fact, it encompasses the ability to accomplish tasks and work at an accelerated pace as well. Superheroes with super speed are fast... bottom line. Because of their super speed, they can finish and accomplish many tasks quickly or faster than the average. Super speed also allows the hero to multitask as well. And, it allows a superhero to adjust to the pace of the battle, situation, or disaster.

This ability prevents panic because it involves thinking at a faster pace, and it allows the hero to process and absorb information faster. Most importantly, it allows them to sort through chaotic situations and see the fast-moving parts.... at a clearer slow pace. Leaders with this ability can put out multiple fires and solve multiple problematic situations. They even appear to be able to control time by causing it to slow down so they can accomplish more things! When there are multiple tasks which must be accomplished, this is the power to have because super speed is the gift of efficiency.

Super-fast superheroes are great team members because of the speed at which they can accomplish tasks and the number of tasks they can work. However, sometimes they move so fast that it's hard to keep track of them! They can also be very impulsive and quick to action, sometimes without thinking long term. A superhero with super speed is very good in chaotic situations and emergency situations. This power is perfect for putting out fires which erupt, but it is a disadvantage for problems that require long-term solutions and a longer investment of time.

14
Extra Sensory Perception (ESP)

Extra Sensory Perception, also known as ESP, is the ability to see patterns and connections other people cannot. This increases the superhero's percentage and probability of solving problems and predicting problems with solutions. A superhero who possesses ESP powers can manifest them in many ways. It can be a combination of a variety of powers or talents which give the superhero heightened sensory abilities. Basically, they are in tune with their environment and all that surrounds them. It gives the superhero the ability of precognition and telepathy or the appearance thereof.

Precognition is the ability to predict upcoming or impending events. Some superheroes are so in sync with their surroundings and environment that they can sense problems and situations that are about to occur in the near future. This is sometimes an early warning system. It allows the superhero to start solving and planning before the problem occurs. Precognition can be developed through experience and the combination of super hearing and super vision.

Leaders with this trait use their super vision to analyze current conditions and situations and then to see situations far off. They use their super hearing to understand the nature of current situations and issues, and then they make the connections between what they hear and what they see. Precognition is basically the prediction and interpretation of outcomes based on the processing and interpretation of the available data that a superhero absorbs from their environment. Based on this data analysis, the superhero can make accurate and high probability predictions. It becomes an extraordinary feat because the superhero processes this information quickly and without much effort.

This superhero ability of telepathy is amazing because it allows leaders to be able to predict what people are thinking and what they are about to do! However, the secret to this ability is the same as precognition: processing and interpreting data. It is possible with some accuracy to predict other people's actions based on what they have done and said in the past and what they are saying and doing in the present. Let's face it, some people are just transparent! Super memory combined with super vision and super hearing allows the hero to recall, see, and hear data about a person.

Again, the trick is that a superhero does this so quickly and effortlessly that it gives the impression that they "read your mind." The ability to process readily available data with speed and accuracy and to make proper adjustments to their course of action based on that data is the key to the ESP powers. Correct interpretation comes from experience and learning. A more seasoned and experienced superhero will be more accurate than a rookie.

It is always good to team up with a superhero with ESP abilities. They can warn you of potential problems. They can suggest alternate routes to your goal or alternate routes to avoid potential peril. They can also help you plan strategically and create good mission actions. In addition, they can provide valuable information about people and their intentions, motives, and trustworthiness. However, this power is not one hundred percent accurate because it relies on the superhero's ability to interpret and process data, and nobody is one hundred percent predictable or accurate.

15

Elemental

In every situation, there are elements that need to be understood or controlled. Elemental power is the ability to control the elements of an environment: fire, water, earth, wind and the weather. These elements make up the atmosphere and climate of every situation. A superhero that is gifted with elemental power can manipulate, feed off, direct, and control the elements that make up an environment. These superheroes possess a strong sense of empathy with the people around them and their environment. They can feel what others feel, and they can understand what they need. Moreover, they can feel the mood of any climate and know what is present, what is lacking, and the dormant or latent potential. These superheroes know almost instinctively what is needed to make an environment grow and flourish. They also know when the environment is in excess, and they can bring everything back into balance.

A superhero with this power can control or influence the environment in which you work or battle. The weather of the environment also can dictate the mood of the people in it. A little rain can help cool tempers and disperse crowds. However, a lot of rain can lead to floods, damage, and depression. A little wind can move smoke and put out fire, but too much can blow everything away, spread flames, and drive people away. The superhero who wields this power must be in control of it and understand how and when to use it. A few rocks can be good for traction when the path has become too smooth, but too many rocks can block the path and make travel difficult. A little brush fire can help cleanse a crowded and thick underbrush, while an uncontrolled wildfire can burn down the whole forest.

A superhero who can control and understand the basic elements can likewise add to the environment and enhance the situation. A leader with these abilities can come into a situation or environment and turn the tide of battle significantly in their favor. Remember you can never completely control an environment, and drastic changes to any environment can be disastrous. A superhero with this ability and strong control of this power is an asset because they can come into any environment or situation and understand what's going on while directing the strengths which are already present. Although these superheroes may have certain areas and environments in which they may feel more comfortable, they can blend and work in even the most hostile of environments. Nothing helps more than being down and out in the pouring rain and then someone on your team brings out the sunshine. How's that for a morale booster!

16
Invisibility

Invisibility is the ability to be virtually unseen. A superhero with this superpower can carry out missions and tasks without being seen or noticed. They do not draw attention to themselves, and they are very subtle in their actions. Not every superhero likes to be seen carrying out their duties. Some superheroes use invisibility so that they can work uninterrupted. They prefer to accomplish tasks without receiving attention, credit, or acknowledgments.

Although a superhero can be invisible, they are not intangible. Just because they're unseen does not mean their presence cannot be felt. A superhero can affect an environment and help change the world without a spotlight or recognition. They complete their missions, affect change, and are hardly noticed. The only drawback for a superhero who chooses to use this power is that no one can follow their lead or example.

"Courage is being scared to death but saddling up anyway."

John Wayne

17

Invincibility

Many superheroes are impervious to many things that would cause the mere mortal harm. Extreme heat or cold, bullets, knives, death rays all seem to do them no harm. Most superheroes have very tough skin, they are very resistant to injury, and they can bounce back and recover quickly from most setbacks. They will continue their mission despite injury, pain, fatigue, or fights through opposition and circumstances which would have crushed ordinary people. This leads to the assumption that superheroes are invincible and that they cannot be hurt. However, this is a huge superhero myth.

No matter the superhero. No matter their skill level. No matter their powers. No matter the battle experience. There is no such thing as total invincibility. Every superhero has a weakness or vulnerability. It is the cosmic check and balance system. Every superhero has something that they are not good at doing. Most superheroes are aware of their weaknesses. They just don't advertise it or play around with it! When they come across their weakness, they may partner up with other superheroes or find other ways to compensate. Only the arrogant superhero believes they are invincible. Still, every superhero has a task or mission they cannot accomplish without the help of someone else. The failure to understand this principle has led to the fall and early retirement of many superhero careers.

"Knowing others is intelligence; knowing yourself is true wisdom. Mastering others is strength; mastering yourself is true power."
Tao Te Ching

SUPERHERO WISDOM

"We thought, because we had power, we had wisdom."
Stephen Vincent Benet

18

THE SUPERHERO LESSONS

All Superheroes benefit from trademark and professional secrets, knowledge, and understanding. Through many adventures and misadventures, an occupational knowledge for superheroes has emerged. This has evolved into a superhero code. Every superhero has learned many lessons as they have waged crusades in the never-ending battle for truth and justice. Part of being a successful leader is learning from your mistakes and success. Repetition of the same mistake is a not a trait of a successful superhero or leader. Even if you are not a full-fledged superhero yet, you can benefit from the wisdom of these superhero lessons. It is the acquisition of knowledge that sets true superheroes apart from the average person and makes them super.

19
Superhero Lessons for Life

1. Always give others a chance to give up and come clean.
2. Mistakes can sometimes erase good deeds.
3. Always be prepared for the unexpected.
4. Good deeds are their own reward.
5. Even superheroes have bad days.
6. Have good mentors.
7. Nobody likes a show-off.
8. Be dependable.
9. Everybody gets beaten sometimes.
10. Have a secret identity.
11. Have modesty and grace when accepting compliments.
12. Always have some power in reserve.
13. Networking is a good thing.
14. Have a good headquarter.
15. Your brain is your best weapon.
16. Dress the part.
17. Be on time.
18. Never give up!
19. Actions speak louder than words.
20. If it was easy, everybody would do it.

1. **Always give others a chance to give up and come clean.**

One of the golden rules of being a superhero is that you must always believe in the good of other people and that there is good in every person. When you accept this basic rule of the superhero profession, you must also give people the opportunity to realize their mistakes or the error of their ways and come clean. A superhero always gives a person the opportunity to discover their mistake, admit their mistake and take responsibility for their actions. Most times, it would be easier to point out the obvious and not give them the opportunity for self-discovery...or admission. However, if you believe in the good in people, then you must provide an opportunity for it to come out. Besides, most times it is far better for people to come to the realization of their mistakes on their own rather than being forced.

Sometimes a person has been backed into a corner by one poor choice or circumstance after another. Assumptions can further push a person into a corner or push them further down the wrong path. Sometimes providing them this opportunity to choose for themselves is the break that they need to make the right choice. One right choice can empower them to make another good choice and then another until they find themselves back on the right path. As a superhero, you always should believe that deep down everyone can make the right choice when given the opportunity. Remember that the superhero business is a people business. Superheroes believe in people.

2. **Mistakes can sometimes erase good deeds.**

No matter how many good deeds a superhero performs. No matter how many good works a superhero can accomplish. No matter how much praise or how many compliments are given to a superhero. No matter how many good words are spoken about a superhero. Sometimes one mistake, one slip up, one bad decision can turn all the good you've done upside down. One bad decision can erase all the good deeds from a superhero supporter's memories and turn their once fans into critics. Trust is fragile. Therefore, when you lose the trust of people, you have to rebuild it from the bottom. Therefore, it is so important to be diligent and thoughtful in your decision making.

Weigh decisions carefully, be alert and always prepared, and give your best effort every time. Mistakes happen. Errors cannot be avoided sometimes. Still, remember that opinions sway like grass in the wind. Never get caught up in compliments or rest on your past good deeds. Always continue to work hard and continue to do what is right. Fight the good fight regardless of popular opinion.

Remember that you are sometimes only as good as your last good deed. So, you should keep moving and finish one task before moving to the next. However, if you betray the trust of the people you serve, it is a different matter. Mistakes can be forgiven. Betrayal is a world breaker.

3. Always be prepared for the unexpected.

The best prepared superheroes often ask themselves, "What if this is the day it all goes bad? If it does, what do I do?" Mentally preparing for the bad situations allows a superhero to better prepare for the unexpected. Training on worse case scenarios before bad things happen can mentally prepare any leader. If you prepare for the chaos (which almost always eventually happens) while everything is calm, you will always be prepared when the chaos breaks out. You will never run out of ammunition during a battle or leave your most valued weapon at headquarters. Most importantly, you will never panic because you have prepared yourself.

The biggest mistake superheroes can make is to think that nothing bad will ever happen. A superhero must always be prepared even when things are going smoothly. They must prepare for the rain while the sun is shining. So, when there is a break in crime, a good superhero is taking inventory, updating his equipment, thinking of new strategies, and training. You cannot predict the unexpected (unless that is your superpower), but you can control how prepared you are for the unexpected.

4. **Good deeds are their own reward because most of the time, nobody knows you saved the world.**

Superheroes must understand that their heroic deeds do not make the evening news often. Ticker tape, parades, and awards are few and far between. As a matter of fact, a good superhero understands that if they do their job correctly, most people will never know that they have done anything anyway. Accordingly, you can't be in this business for the accolades or recognition. This is sometimes the difficult part of the job. You train hard, battle hard, and achieve a great victory over insurmountable odds. But, in your elation, you look around and no one knows or noticed! Either no one was watching, or they were too consumed with their own lives to notice or care. Superheroes should remain focused on the fact that we do the things we do because we have the ability and because it is the right thing to do. We are not superheroes for monetary compensation, recognition, award, perks, or even for a thank you. On a good day, nobody is going to even know that you saved the world. The next day, you may have to do it all over again – still without being noticed. We are superheroes because we can do it.

5.   Even superheroes have bad days.

People think just because you wear a cape and can deflect bullets that you never have a bad day. Even superheroes have bad days. Those are the days when everything goes wrong. We all have days when we wake up late, forget something important, or get stuck in traffic (if you can't fly!). We all have days when our best plans backfire, misfire, or just don't work. We run into rude, mean, and ungrateful people. We all have the days when the job is too demanding and everybody needs saving all at once. Nevertheless, what defines a superhero is the ability to push through those days and still get the job done.

Everybody has a stressful day occasionally. So, don't be fooled into thinking that just because you are a superhero, every day will be smooth sailing. The difference is that superheroes keep going and keep fighting. If the leaders quit, then we let down those who need us and depend on us the most. Besides, when superheroes do not perform their jobs, everyone else will have an even worse day!

6. Have good mentors.

The superhero profession can be tough to master, and the learning curve can be steep even for the most talented hero. Sometimes you need someone to show you the ropes or give you ideas or suggestions on getting better. Everybody needs a good mentor, especially if you are new to the game of saving the world. Every successful superhero has been mentored, trained, guided, and counseled by someone stronger, wiser, or more talented. It is important that you have a good mentor because they pass on valuable knowledge and experience about the field and career path. If you have a mentor who is not contributing to your overall well-being, that person should be replaced. You cannot live long enough to experience everything, but mentors can give you the benefit of their experiences and adventures. It doesn't take super hearing to listen to a mentor and learn.

7. Nobody likes a show-off.

In general, no one likes a show-off. Superheroes are all gifted with great abilities. They range from great to small to extraordinary to ordinary. However, no one superhero's gift is greater or better than anyone else's gift or talent. Superheroes use their gifts to get the job done and save the day. People are impressed with a leader who does his job. It doesn't have to be pretty, elaborate, or super stylish.

However, no one likes being made to feel small or insignificant by your gift. Being a show off in this profession does not make you a superhero... It makes you a super zero.

8. Be dependable.

What good is a superhero if the people can't depend on them? No good of course! If the city or company calls for you and they can't count on you to show up, then why should they call? This is what separates the average from the super; we are dependable. We have the confidence of the people. Our name is synonymous with dependability and reliability. We inspire confidence. Every knows that a superhero will show up whenever we are needed. Furthermore, when we show up, the job will get done. No matter if the job is big or small or if the task is easy or difficult, superheroes come with our "A" game. There is never a doubt when the signal flare is shot, the beacon is lit, or the red phone is dialed. We will be there.

9. Everybody gets beaten sometimes, but you don't have to like it.

The law of averages applies to everyone, including superheroes. For every good time, there will be bad times. There is no superhero with an undefeated record or unblemished battle history. You will lose sometimes. It will happen. There is always that bad guy who got away. There will always be that time you got outsmarted. There will be the time when you were simply flat out beat! Superheroes get beat too, but we don't have to like it.

When superheroes get beaten or defeated, we get up, dust ourselves off, and get back into the fight. We learn lessons from our losses so that they are not repeated...at least not the same way. Our defeats don't defeat us. Rather, they inspire us and motivate us to get better, stronger, and more powerful. Sometimes it is after a defeat that a superhero finds that our power has increased, evolved, or we have developed new powers. Superheroes get better and evolve to higher levels after each defeat. We may lose a battle, but the war is never lost unless we quit.

10. Everybody needs a secret identity.

Even though the battles may be never-ending, every superhero needs an occasional break. This is why it is mandatory for every superhero to have a secret identity. The secret identity allows you to get away from the action for a while. If you don't have a secret identity you are under the spotlight twenty-four hours a day seven days a week. And, no one can hold up to that pressure! Battles can be fierce and can go on for long periods of time. In addition, many projects require extra hours and overtime. Thus, everybody needs a vacation, a break, or mental holiday. All work and no play makes a superhero not so super and definitely not a lot of fun to be around. Moreover, extended time in superhero mode can lead to prolonged stress and fatigue. Prolonged stress and fatigue do not help a superhero, and it can interfere with their abilities and judgment.

The secret identity provides you with balance between being a superhero and living life. You have to live life to appreciate it, and you have to appreciate life to help others. Take time for yourself every now and then. Rest and relaxation give a superhero a fresh perspective on things. Get a hobby or find side interests. Secret identities allow you to remember why saving the world is so important.

11. Have modesty and grace when accepting compliments.

As a superhero, there will plenty of times when people will compliment you on a job well done. Many times, people will be impressed with the job that you do and your fantastic abilities. Because of this, sometimes a superhero may find themselves being showered by compliments. However, the shower will slow to a trickle, and then to a drip if a superhero does not know how to accept compliments! We must have modesty and grace when accepting compliments. A superhero must shy away from too much praise because they would never be able to get any work done.

Arrogance is the fall of many would-be superheroes. Compliments can be seductive and addictive. Remember that a leader does not work for praise and glamour. And, everyone that compliments you is not on your side. Some compliments and smiles can hide sinister intentions and ulterior motives. Beware of flows of compliments and flattery. It can be a huge distraction from your superhero mission. Besides, while a superhero is on stages receiving awards and in parades in your honor, who is out saving the world? Refrain from long speeches, bowing, and shout outs. The superhero standard reply of "Thank you" and a quick departure is highly recommended.

12. Always have some power in reserve.

Every superhero should know this rule. Every battle is like a high stakes poker game. You have to know when to hold them, fold them, and show your cards. You never show all your cards in the beginning! There are always villains and enemies who are watching, measuring, and gauging what you can and can't do. Superheroes should use just enough power to get the job done. If you keep some in reserve, you will always surprise your future enemies and break their expectations.

Sometimes a superhero's mission will throw unexpected curves. There will be complications that you have not planned for and changes of circumstances that you did not anticipate. If you have some energy left in reserve, you can still handle the unexpected and still complete your mission. Always keep some for the fourth quarter push, the two-minute warning, and the final countdown. Pace yourself so you can finish every battle strong.

13. Stay Fresh: Networking is a good thing.

It is not possible to be everywhere and see everything. It is also impossible to know all the new innovations and techniques in the superhero game. Moreover, it's hard to keep up with all the new superheroes, new villains, balances of power, superhero regulations, and equipment. Networking is a must in the superhero business. You must surround yourself with other superheroes and share information. Sometimes other leaders have answers to problems that you are experiencing, or perhaps they can lend a helping hand when things get out of control. It is good to attend conferences, summits, or gatherings when other superheroes are getting together. The exchange of ideas can be great and refreshing. There is never any value in re-inventing the wheel.

Talented people share ideas and help each other to get better. The sharing of ideas promotes growth and understanding. Isolation breeds stagnation and places a person out of touch with the pace of the rest of the world. Good networking also helps create a support structure for you by giving you superheroes to call on when you need help, have questions, or just need to vent. A good network can be your motivation, your encouragement, and your inspiration. Stay fresh. Get a good network.

14. Have a good Headquarters.

All superheroes need a base of operation, even if it's just to have a place to hang your cape and get some shut-eye. However, a base of operation is and can be much more. Your headquarters is the place where you begin and end your journey and your adventures. It is the place at the center of your mission and the place where your strategies are created. A headquarters is vital to the productive work of a superhero.

Not everyone can afford the same size or the same square footage for a headquarter, but the size of the place does not matter. Whether it is a luxury state of the art facility, a garage, or a basement, it does not matter. A superhero's workspace should fit your needs no matter the size if it's well-organized. Being organized makes your job more efficient and makes work you more productively. The headquarters should provide a respite from your battles while still providing you the inspiration for the next adventure. In addition, it should house all the things you need to conduct your business. A good headquarters gives you the space to be creative and freedom to explore ideas of how to achieve your max. Nevertheless, it should be the place where you cool your jets, recharge, re-energize, unwind, and get refocused

15. Despite all your great powers and gadgets, you will eventually have to rely on your natural skills.

In the superhero game, it is easy to become reliant on gadgets and technology, especially when there is so much good technology being developed. It is also very easy to rely heavily on our superpowers to get us through every situation. That's what's great about having those, right? Well, the downside is that there comes a point in every superhero's career when he comes upon a bad situation where technology fails or he is simply out of ammo! There is also the time when you come across the occasional supervillain or situation for which our powers do not work, they have been neutralized, or they are inadequate by themselves. There will be a supervillain who has accounted for all your gear, gadgets, gimmicks, and powers. What do you do when time comes? Are you beat? Are you vanquished? Of course, not!

A superhero must rely on the one power that can never be taken from you... your superhero mind. Your mind is the ultimate computer and superpower if you know how to use it! That's why it is crucial that as you train your skills, your physical powers and gifts, you also train and feed your mind. No enemy can ever truly compensate for what you know. Think your way out of situations. Some they require finesse. You can't always blast your way through! Education is essential, and reading is fundamental to personal growth. One should never stop learning and never outgrow the need for additional training, education, or more understanding. When all else has been stripped away, you are only left with what is inside your brain. And, if you have neglected your mental and intellectual training, you may truly be empty-handed.

16. Dress the part.

If you are going to be a superhero, you must dress for the role. This will differ from superhero to superhero since there is no hero standard for dress. Some prefer capes and masks, while others do not. Regardless, your dress should fit you, your ability, and most importantly, your environment. Your uniform should never distract from your purpose or be a liability to your work. Style is great, but sometimes flashy and trendy is not what you need. If people laugh every time you show up or they just stop, stare, and point, you may need a uniform change. If people whisper, hide their eyes, and seem offended as you walk by, you may need a uniform change.

Your uniform should reflect your commitment and dedication to your job and to your mission.

17. Be on time.

Late superheroes are not of any use or any good to anyone. When there is a call, it is usually urgent. Unless speed is your gift, you must plan and coordinate so that you are on time. Showing up after the battle is over usually lands you on the zero list really fast. Quick and prompt response times are a superhero's trademark. Furthermore, completing missions by designated due dates adds to a superhero's credibility.

18. Surround yourself with the best team possible.

We all have been faced with situations that have required us to request the help of our team. Face it, we can't always do it all. So, when the time arrives to assemble a team for a mission, you must assemble the best team as possible.

Surrounding yourself with the best people, even if they are better, stronger, and more talented, is the smartest move you can make! Choose not only people who can get the job done, but people who can inspire you to do your best, be your best, and get better. Remember there is strength in diversity.

19. Never Give up!

Superheroes are leaders for one reason. No matter how hard the job, no matter how big the obstacles, no matter how great the odds, superheroes never give up. They may get beat, but they are never beaten. Superheroes may lose, but they are not losers. They push on and push through. When others quit, superheroes never surrender. This means that sometimes a superhero battles alone, in the dark, and numerous enemies. Sometimes they may even be outnumbered. Still, they understand that victory is achieved through perseverance and that perseverance is rewarded with victory. Superheroes fight through fatigue, negativity, and through all obstacles. This is what separates them from the average. It's not about the gifts or the talents, but the sheer determination and resilience. The greatest power of any superhero is their heart.

20. If it was easy, everybody would do it.

This is the mantra for all superheroes on difficult days or in moments when it would be easy to just whine and complain. The phrase should be engraved on every piece of equipment, hung on the walls of every headquarters, and written on every business card as a reminder of why superheroes consider their jobs. Superheroes do the job, accept the missions, complete the tasks because they are difficult, and it takes someone special to handle them.

When things become difficult and the mission gets hard, superheroes have to pause and tell themselves, "This is why I signed on, and this is what I was made to do!" Leaders do the tasks that seem overwhelming, hard, difficult, and impossible to everyone else. They step up when others pass by and overlook things. The superhero is not built for easy times. They excel in the rough times, at the difficult tasks. Easy is for everyone else.

THE VILLAINS

"Friends may come and go, but enemies accumulate."

Thomas Jones

20

Villain Profiles

Villain - A dramatic character that is typically at odds with the hero.

During doing their duty, a superhero will come across individuals who will make their job difficult. Those are the ones who will attempt to sabotage or foil the superhero's plan or mission. These persons are often referred to as villains. Villains, like the superheroes, range in diversity, skill, and motivation. They can show up anywhere at any time. They can even show up within your team, alliance, network, or circle of friends. The following profiles are designed to help you identify and understand some types of villains a superhero may encounter.

Just as there are no absolutes for superhero personalities, there are no absolutes when it comes to villains. Not all villains are purely bad and uncooperative. Some villains need to be defeated while others need to be converted. They can be roadblocks in your path or the monkey wrench in your plans. They can be fierce animals ready to attack, or they can be the annoying buzzing insect flying around your head. While some villains can eventually become allies or better yet superheroes, others want to battle with you indefinitely. One step to understanding a villain is trying to understand their motivations.

They often make achieving your goal difficult, but not impossible. A villain can only defeat you if you give them the means to do so by surrendering. This section will help you to deal and address each villain appropriately.

21
The Ego Maniacs

The nature of a superhero is selflessness. They take pride in performing and achieving a mission outside of themselves without need of reward, glory, praise, or gratitude. In order words, they serve others and a greater good outside of themselves. Therefore, it is reasonable to believe the opposite for a person consumed with self. The self-centered person is one who acts only in the best interest of self, to the benefit of self, and for the reward, the glory, the praise, and acknowledgment. This is the nature of the Egomaniac villain.

The Egomaniac villain may or may not stand in opposition to the hero. They could even be on the same team! The individual can even be charming, entertaining, and likable at times. It doesn't matter which side of an issue they are on, they are only concerned with what will bring them the most attention - good or bad. It's all about them! They may not be a very tough, destructive, or particularly evil foe, but they can surely slow down progress and become a huge distraction!

Some Egomaniacs can be converted if you can show them the value of others such as teamwork, compassion, charity, etc. One of the best ways to deal with this villain who is in the way of your mission (besides direct confrontation) is to simply deprive them of what drives them the most... attention! Direct confrontation often brings more attention to them. Remember, they thrive off attention. Ignoring them completely can be a very effective strategy.

22

The Wounded Wronged Souls (W.W.S.)

Everyone has been beaten, hurt by someone, wronged, and suffered a miscarriage of justice. That's life! Most of us, after a period of time, get over it and move on with our lives. This is not the case with this villain. This villain did not get over it and refused to move on past what they consider their great injustice. These villains spend all their time and efforts focusing on past errors performed on them by others that they just can't seem to let it go. They can cause a major roadblock to progress and mission plans. They can be like the slow driver holding up traffic behind them. In addition, they can create a negative and toxic environment for others. Negativity and pessimism are tools of this villain. One event or a series of events has caused them to develop such a negative attitude that they cannot move into the positive of the present or future. After some time without redirection, this villain evolves into another villain …The Bitter!

23

The Bitter

At this stage, the W.W.S. villain is perhaps the most difficult to deal with, convert, or reason with because of some shortcoming, disappointment, failure in their life, and their failure to deal with the issue. They have turned bitter and given up on the positive or possibility of good things happening in their lives, they want everybody to know it. This villain could have been a superhero. However, because of some reason, bad defeats, loss, or disappointments and their failure to cope with the problem, they turned their back on their talents and deeds.

Pessimism is what this villain embraces. They will sabotage, block, or disrupt positive activities covertly or openly. They will be the dissenting voice in a room of consent. They will be the sour note in a chorus of praise. They will be the ballot of doubt in a majority vote of confidence. The Bitter is the evolution of the Wounded Wronged. It is the result of an extended time dwelling in the past and not moving forward.

24

The Misunderstood, Confused, Misinformed (M.C.M.)

Sometimes you will find that some villains are not really villains at all. When you encounter some would-be villains, you find them to be capable, skillful, and talented people. If you take time to understand them and their motivations, some people fall into the category of the misunderstood, misinformed, or just confused. They can be a hindrance or obstacle in the way of your mission, but there is often no real intent or master plan to do so. There are times when people are just simply misunderstood.

Most misunderstandings develop from unclear communication, false or misleading information, and failure to ask questions. When a person's intentions are not interpreted clearly, it often results in a blunder, hurt feelings, a disaster, or bad blood. Some people have dry, off-color humor. Others just cannot express themselves correctly. Some people are poor communicators, while others fail to ask the questions that will provide clarity. They may have the best of intentions, but their action results in a catastrophe. Misunderstood people may be able to help your mission and become a positive contributor if you give them the chance and take the opportunity to understand them. To take this step, you must rely on an ancient superhero technique called patience. Applying patience to your skill set allows you to see and understand the true intentions of the misunderstood and the reasons why they are misunderstood.

The Misinformed and Confused people are simply responding to the wrong information. The wrong or misleading information can be about the purpose of your mission, about who you are, your professional record, or your intent. Therefore, their actions are going against the mission or the goal based on bad or incomplete information. This misinformation can come from a lack of communication on your part or misleading information from another hidden villain. Sometimes there are other villains who rely on the Misinformed and Confused to run interference with superheroes and to also distract people from what deeds and tasks they are doing. If you give this person the correct information, provide them with clarity, or allow them to get answers to their questions, they will cease being a villain. In fact, you may find yourself with a new strong ally.

25

Under a Bad Influence

These are individuals who have fallen in with a bad crowd or under the influence of the wrong people. There are villains who take on the ideas of the people around them. They agree and go along with the plans, schemes, and ideas of others even if deep down they do not agree or think the same. These villains are your Villains Under a Bad Influence (UBI).

How did these individuals fall under a bad influence? There can be many reasons why this happens, and each reason might be different and unique to each person. Some UBI villains may feel the need to fit into a certain group for acceptance. Some may feel a misplaced sense of loyalty based on a past act of kindness. Other UBI villains may lack the confidence to stand alone or be alone. And, there are other UBI villains who have subordinate personalities and fall under the influence of villains with more dominant personalities. People with more perceived experience or skill can also dominate persons with seemingly less experience or skills.

When a superhero identifies a UBI villain, divide and conquer is the best strategy for dealing with this type of villain. This villain alone may not be a bad person or villain at all. They can often be reasoned with, converted, and placed on the right path when they are on their own. When separated from the bad influences, the villain's own sense of right and wrong will begin to emerge, and the value system which is right and true for them will come to the surface. If you can empower them to stand on their own, show them a better way, or convince them to trust their own thoughts and beliefs, a superhero can turn a UBI villain into a great ally or better yet… a superhero.

26

The Phantom Villain

There are some situations when you can get the distinct feeling that despite the problem before you, there is something that you're not seeing. When you confront the MCM villains and sometimes the UBI villains, you can get the sense that there is another person or other people involved that you cannot see. When all the clues and problems point to the fact that there is some other unseen force working against you, you may be encountering the work of a Phantom villain. The Phantom Villain can be the most dangerous villain of them all.

This villain is usually lurking in the shadows, pulling stings from afar, and throwing stones from a safe distance. A Phantom Villain will never confront a superhero directly. Instead, they use other villains and people to do their work. From the safety of the shadows, they spread misinformation, gossip, lies, half-truths, and doubt to anyone that will listen. They rely on the MCM and the UBI. They can use the Bitter villains as well.

Whenever you discover or feel that you are battling a Phantom villain, it is imperative that you find and expose them as soon as possible. A Phantom villain left alone to work hidden in the shadows can reap havoc on your mission and plans. This individual can recruit and turn people against you, put obstacles in your path, and create an army of villains to thwart your plans at every turn. The worst part is that it will be done with no risk or harm on their part. They villain strike from anywhere, and they can even be hidden on your team.

Begin exposing a Phantom by retracing the clues and trail left behind. Follow the trail of misinformation back to the sources. By bringing the Phantom villain to the light, you can neutralize their power and bring the number of villains in your path to a reasonable number. The Phantom villain's strength and power lie in their ability to be unseen and to be far away from the mayhem they create.

27
Lessons from Villains

One important lesson that all superheroes learn is that you can learn from everyone…even your enemies! Every battle gives you more insight, clues, and information that can be used in future engagements. Super villains are a good source of information because they can be highly predictable if you pay close attention. You must know your enemies better than they know you. When you do this, you can sway the odds of victory decisively in your favor. Remember there is wisdom in the mistakes of others, the decisions they make, and the consequences which arise because of their choices. Learning these lessons and applying them can prevent you from committing the same mistakes. Moreover, it can help you avoid the same or similar pitfalls.

"The wise learn many things from their enemies."

Aristophanes

28

The Villain Lessons

1. Talk is cheap.
2. Don't procrastinate.
3. Most of the people you are mad at don't know it.
4. Move on.
5. Be aware of how you treat people. Grudges can last a long time.
6. There is no honor among thieves.
7. Know when to cut your losses.

1. Talk is cheap

Villains tend to talk endlessly about their plans for domination and victory. It is these long rants that often give them the opportunities needed to prevail. When given the chance, sometimes villains will spend far more time outlining a plan and bragging of what will be accomplished. However, they will never get around to doing any of it. This is what superheroes count on when dealing with super villains because talk is cheap.

We all have met people who talk too much. Those are the people who spend a lot of time chatting about all the things they can do, have done, or will do. In fact, they spend more time talking than actually producing. If you want to impress people, produce! What you produce is what counts, and it is how people will judge you. Too much time spent talking about what you will do only allows someone else to do it first, do it better, or to sabotage your attempts. It is best to let your actions speak for you. Besides, actions always speak louder than words.

The shaft of the arrow had been feathered with one of the eagle's own plumes. We often give our enemies the means of our own destruction."
Aesop, The Eagle and the Arrow

2. Don't Procrastinate. Finish the job.

Many superheroes have been saved by a villain's sense of procrastination. Every superhero has found themselves captured and on the verge of ultimate defeat by a villain. However, instead of finishing the job, the villain decides to wait, keep the superhero around to watch, to keep them around to brag, or just gets preoccupied with something else. This procrastination always gives a superhero the time to recover their strength, to plot their escape, and to figure out how to defeat the villain's ultimate plan.

Do not procrastinate. Finish a job or task completely before moving on to another one. Loose ends tend to come back and bite you or defeat you. When you hesitate, it creates an opportunity for other people to snatch away your victory. Do the job completely and thoroughly. Don't share this wisdom with the villains!

3. Most of the people you are mad at don't know it.

In every superhero story, there is one villain that appears to settle an old score with the superhero. This villain is driven by the passion for revenge and vengeance by some act done against him in the past. In the mind of the villain, this act was so rude, horrible, demeaning, and underhanded that it has made them spend years of their life, time, and effort to get back at the person. When the moment finally arrives, the other person does not even remember them or the act that has set them in motion!

When someone wronged a villain in the past it made them mad, angry, or upset. They decided to remain angry until they could get their revenge! However, the thing about revenge is that it is time-consuming. It requires a lot of attention, time, commitment, and resources. Villains end up spending much of their energy, time, and thoughts on making someone pay, only to realize in the end that the person of their fixation is not even aware of what they did to incur the anger or payback.

When you feel that someone has done you wrong, disrespected you, been rude, or hurt your feelings, confront that person immediately or as soon as possible. Let them know how you feel. Most likely, it was unintentional or an oversight on their part or even a misunderstanding. Holding on to being mad only hurts the person that is holding onto it. In most cases, the other person does not know and sometimes just doesn't care!

4. "Move on."

Every superhero runs across a villain that was not always a super villain. At one point, they were a normal person going through life like everyone else. Life was good until one day some unforeseen incident happened and changed everything. Instead of moving on with their life, they let the incident consume their life. They never forgot. They chose to dwell in self-pity, grief, and bitterness. The person they once were became lost, and they warped into a villain determined to inflict their pain on everyone else. Don't let this happen to you. Move on.

Life is filled with many unexpected twists and turns. Many things happen that we can never plan for or protect against. Life is unpredictable. While there are many bad things that can happen, there are also many, many good things that can happen as well. We can only control how we react to the situations that we are dealt. Move on. Don't let situations or circumstances change who you are or destroy your life. If you let the bad things dominate your thoughts and blur your vision, you will miss out on all the good things coming into view just over the horizon. Remember only you are in control of your happiness… or the lack thereof.

5. **Be aware of how you treat people. Grudges can last a long time.**

In life, there are people who like you, and there are also people who just do not like you. We know some of these people (and we know why they don't like us, if we are honest). Some of them, we do not know, and we will never have a clue why they do not like us. So, when the time comes for us to pay, we are at a loss and blindsided by the one-sided grudge.

Grudges do not need our acknowledgment to be validated. They can simply be started by small acts such as being disrespectful towards someone, rudeness, being ungrateful, or not acknowledging people. A one-sided grudge can grow all by itself. Most times, sadly but truly, these battles could have been diffused a long time ago by a simple "Thank you." or "I'm sorry."

It is much easier to acknowledge those people you encounter daily. It is very important to be mindful of how you treat others because grudges can last a long time. In addition, be mindful of how you speak to people. It is such a very simple act to say, "I'm sorry." "Thank you." "Good morning." When you treat people wrong, you never know how or when you will encounter them again. Politeness, kind words, and common courtesy go a long way. And, they can be more powerful than any superpower.

6. **There is no honor among thieves.**

If you partner with other people to achieve a mission, no matter how good a plan is conceived or how talented the people are it will not work out and the mission will not be achieved if they lack morals and character. Most likely, you will come out on the bad end of the deal and in a far worse situation than when you started. People with no character or people whose intentions are not morally centered cannot be trusted. The offer may look good and the rewards may sound good, but it is all glitter and no gold. If someone is dubious and immoral towards other people, what makes you so sure that they will not do the same to you? This is a fatal flaw with villains. The super villain teams and alliance may be formidable and powerful, but they eventually crumble because they cannot trust each other or work together without self-interest surfacing.

7. Know when to cut your losses.

Most villains know how and when to make a hasty retreat. They recognize when the tide of battle has turned and when it is time to throw in the towel. They can recognize when it is better to retreat and live to fight another day. Superheroes need to learn this lesson as well. We need to be able to recognize when to cut our losses and when to regroup.

In a battle, superheroes must understand when the losses would be greater than the gains. At those times, we don't quit. We just need to pull a strategic retreat. No superhero likes the idea of retreat, but sometimes it is a better option than a severely devastating lost that could be avoided.

Retreat does not equal defeat. Regrouping does not mean quitting.

"Never interrupt your enemy when he is making a mistake."

Napoleon Bonaparte

THE SIDEKICKS SECTION: FOR SUPERHEROES IN TRAINING

"Even when walking in the company of two other men, I am bound to be able to learn from them. The good points of the one I copy; the bad points of the other I correct in myself."
Confucius

29

The Superhero-in-training

A superhero-in-training is often referred to as a sidekick. This superhero works with or under someone else (a mentor) who they consider to be a great superhero role model. They learn how to be a superhero by working under the supervision of someone with the experience. Eventually, every superhero should go out on his own to stand and fight. However, to be a good superhero you must have some good basic fundamentals training.

The superhero-in-training is paired or apprenticed under another superhero. They are in the position to learn and gather valuable information and training. The sidekick usually does not have to worry about the spotlight of attention because it is typically focused on their superhero mentor. This allows them to fully observe, watch, and learn from their mentor. The sidekick gets to participate in battles, adventures, and misadventures without the burden of the success or failure resting solely on them. Often there are many a superhero who wish they could go back to this stage! A sidekick does have the ability to contribute to a mission and can help to save the day. Most of the time, they defer to their mentor and then they stand back to watch, learn, and grow in experience and power.

30
Tips for Superheroes in Training

1. Find a good mentor
2. Put in the necessary work and effort.
3. Learn the trade not just the tricks of the trade.
4. Never be afraid to ask questions.
5. Listen, watch, and learn everything you can.
6. Accept solo projects and assignments when given the opportunity.
7. Treat every experience good or bad as a learning opportunity.
8. Persevere.

1. Find a good mentor

This is very important if you want to do the job right. To be a good superhero, you have to learn the job the right way from the right person. To be the best, you must learn from the best. Every aspiring or beginning superhero needs to have a good superhero mentor. They need guidance and help with direction. A good mentor will also help a mentee develop into a superhero in their own right. Moreover, they will encourage you while providing the necessary instruction, guidance, and skills to become a great leader.

2. Put in the necessary work and effort.

There is no way around it, and there is no way to avoid it. If you want to be great, you must put in the necessary work and effort. In some careers, they call this the "paying your dues" stage. It means to be a full-fledged superhero or to be on top one day, you must earn it by working hard and putting in the time and effort. Learning a skill or completing a task may take long hours of practice and many hours of sacrifice. However, as you gain experience, tasks become easier because you will become stronger and more conditioned.

3. Learn the trade not just the tricks of the trade.

In every profession, there are secrets of the trade, tricks of the trade, or shortcuts. However, a successful career cannot be made and sustained on shortcuts alone. Every shortcut and trick of the trade is founded on longer and more detailed processes and procedures. It is the understanding of these procedures and processes that make the difference. There are some situations in which the trick will not work. When faced with such a situation, you have to rely on the original process. If you never learned the long process or procedure and lack the understanding of the whole, you will be stuck without an option. The only way to learn the trade is to go back to rule number two and "put in the necessary work and effort!"

4.   Never be afraid to ask questions.

Ignorance is a temporary state of being that we can dwell in or leave behind at any time. Most of the time, it only takes us to ask the right questions to gain proper knowledge. There are no superheroes who are all knowing or hold all the answers. At some point, we run into things we do not know or understand or need some clarifications. Asking questions is essential. Doing so does not reflect weakness. Instead, it reflects the desire to understand. Asking questions allows a superhero to gather the correct information and understand the task ahead. Making decisions and devising strategies from the state of ignorance can have costly results. Information is key to acquiring the right knowledge to make the best decisions. Never be afraid to ask questions. Sometimes our assumptions are wrong, and we end up missing the point entirely.

5.   Listen, watch, and learn everything you can.

When learning to be a superhero, learn everything you can. As you start out, it'll be hard to predict which lessons will be very important to your superhero career. It is difficult to know what missions you will accept or what type of obstacles you will encounter. By learning as much as you can, it makes you better prepared for the unknown. Although the current task or topic before you may be tedious or boring, you never know when it will be valuable to you in the future.

6. Accept solo projects and assignments when given the opportunity.

Eventually, every sidekick will have the opportunity go on to be a superhero. The best way to train for the day you will handle the full responsibility of a mission on your own is to practice. As a sidekick, practice by taking on small tasks and solo projects whenever you get the opportunity. These solo projects and assignments are ways for you to grow and learn in a real-time situation. The best thing about solo projects and assignments is that it allows you to form your own superhero style and establish your superhero powers. While you are a sidekick, you still have a mentor to guide you and help you out in a jam. Also, your mentor can talk you through your mistakes and teach you better techniques while giving you positive feedback. Take advantage of this opportunity to expand your training and skill.

7. Treat every experience, good or bad, as a learning opportunity.

Just like any other trade or career, on the path to being a superhero, you will have many experiences. Some of the experiences will be good, and some of them will be bad. However, a good sidekick who wants to be a good superhero will look at all experiences as learning experiences. Every experience is a chance to grow, learn, get better, and most importantly become wiser.

One of the strengths of a good superhero is their outlook on life and situations. Even in bad situations when things do not turn out as planned and the outcome is nothing as imagined, there lies the opportunity to learn and to get better. Sometimes it is easy to learn from our bad experiences than our good because we really want to avoid repeating the bad experiences. The ultimate test is if you can learn from the good experiences as well. Identifying the factors and components of good experiences can help you be able to reproduce them.

8.   Persevere.

Superheroes do not quit. Therefore, if you aspire to be a superhero, you cannot quit either. You have to push through the tough stuff and bad situations. You must work through the difficult and complex things. You may not be the best yet. You may not be the strongest yet. You may not be the wisest yet, but you still must persevere. You cannot always control the circumstances, the obstacles, or the tasks, but you can always control whether you will preserve to the end.

31
FOR SUPERHERO
MENTORS

No superhero can live and fight forever. It is the responsibility of current superheroes to help train future superheroes. It is important for leaders to pass on their knowledge, skills, and professional knowledge, and to motivate the next generation of superheroes. In order to ensure that there are always superheroes to carry on the never-ending fight, current superheroes must mentor upcoming leaders.

When the time comes that you must move on, retire, or pass the torch you should have someone waiting who can handle the handoff. It's in the best interest of superheroes everywhere to give sidekicks the best training possible. Eventually, sidekicks become full-fledged superheroes. Therefore, you want them to be prepared to ensure that they have a long productive career. Sidekicks can either be the superheroes of tomorrow or worst, the villains of tomorrow. So, they should be handled with care and respect and trained well, not just dumped on. Remember a superhero reflects the leaders who trained them!

32
Tips for Superheroes Who Mentor

1. Know how to identify potential.
2. Share your actual experiences.
3. Guide them, show them, teach them but don't force them.
4. Be patient.
5. Listen to their concerns, issues, questions, and goals.
6. Teach them the basics before the advance stuff.
7. Don't spoil all the mysteries.
8. Allow them to make their own mistakes.
9. Be a mentor, not taskmaster.
10. Help them get exposure and experience.

1. Know how to identify potential.

A good mentor superhero knows how to spot potential and talent. If cultivated, nurtured, and grown, those attributes can lead to pure superhero talent. A good mentor can spot and identify the potential and abilities of a person sometimes before they can. When talent is identified early, it can be guided and trained properly. Wasted potential does no one any good. If a superhero cannot spot young talent and potential talent, then a villain will. Young potential is fragile and can be easily influenced, encouraged, or discouraged. Being a good superhero means being on the lookout and keeping your eye out for the new talent, potential, and future superheroes.

2. Share your actual experiences.

When mentoring a potential superhero, superhero-in-training, or sidekick, it is important to share your experiences. A sidekick or superhero-in-training can have unrealistic views of their career choice and path. They may have unclear thoughts of how to use their talents and the obstacles they will face. The best way to help them understand and form their own mission and true path is to share your real-life experiences. Your actual experiences can be much better than the textbook or stereotypical experiences that they may read or dream about. It is great for a superhero-in-training to know and understand the technical aspects of being a superhero, but it is also very important for them to understand that everybody's experience will be different. Most importantly, they need to see that every adventure does not go according to the plan.

3. Guide them, show them, and teach them... but don't force them.

As a mentor, it is very important not to push a mentee into our path or a chosen profession. Our role is to guide sidekicks and show them what being a superhero is all about. However, in the end, it is their choice to become a superhero or not. The role of superhero should not be forced on anyone. A person must choose to be a leader. If someone chooses this role for the wrong reasons, they will not last in the profession for long. If a person lacks the skills, the will, the drive, or the heart, they can do more damage than good.

4. Be patient.

When mentoring and teaching a superhero-in-training, patience is a must. Patience allows the mentor to encourage the potential talent without shattering confidence. Sometimes mentors can push too hard and expect too much too soon from potential superheroes. Tolerance allows a mentor to reflect and remember that experience cannot be gained all at once. The ultimate goal of mentoring is to bring out the best in the mentee, not the worst.

5. Listen to their concerns, issues, questions, and goals.

One of the many roles of a mentor is to become a good listener. Always allow your mentee to ask questions and to feel comfortable asking them. When you listen to questions and concerns, you can better understand their thought process and how to better guide them. Also, you can better assess what types of experiences and training they may need. Listening provides a clear path of communication and relieves confusion, frustrations, and potential mistakes.

6. **Teach them the basics before the advanced stuff.**

A good mentor knows that there is a natural order to learning and growing as a superhero. In order to build sustainable skills and power gains, a mentor must know how to start a mentee off with achievable tasks and skills. If you have a talented mentee, it may be tempting to give them advanced lessons before the basic ones. Still, it is important to cover the basics of superhero skills before jumping into the advanced techniques. Some mentees will move through tasks faster and mature into leaders faster than others. However, giving advanced techniques to your mentees before they are ready could have a reverse effect. If a mentee is given advanced techniques prematurely, they could damage their career and mission. Advanced techniques work only with the understanding that comes with practice and the accompanying skills. Without understanding, advanced techniques can be applied at the wrong time or in the wrong situation. This can lead to defeats, embarrassing losses, and career setbacks.

7. **Don't spoil all the mysteries.**

There are some surprises which make being a superhero enjoyable. Then, there are some experiences that you have to just work through yourself to gain knowledge and an appreciation of a task. As mentors, sometimes you want to tell your mentee everything. Other times, it is best to let them discover some things on their own. Prepare them for their journey, but don't spoil all the nice surprises and moments of discovery which await them. What good is a great adventure or mystery novel, if you know all the twists and turns in the plot before you begin?

8. Allow them to make their own mistakes.

Trying to avoid and prevent all mistakes from happening is like trying to prevent the sun from rising and setting… It is not going to happen! There has not been a superhero alive who has avoided making at least one mistake, and there will never be one who does. Mistakes are a part of life; we all make them. As much as we try to avoid them, sometimes they are essential for us to learn and get better at what we do. If we understand what can go wrong, it makes for more careful decision-making and increases the odds of making better decisions in the future.

9. Be a mentor, not taskmaster.

Having a sidekick involves much more than delegating monotonous and mundane tasks and duties. Some people feel that the assigning of tasks and duties alone is sufficient to train a mentee. If the job could be learned by doing alone, there would be no need for mentors. Being a good mentor includes guiding and advising. A good mentor must be ready to explain the meaning, purpose, and objectives behind tasks and assignments. Taking the time to make sure that a sidekick understands the value of the lessons will help ensure that they comprehend and advance their training.

10. Help them get exposure and experience.

A good superhero mentor will expose their mentee to the world of the superhero and help them get as much experience as possible. A good mentor understands that they do not have all the answers to all the questions that a mentee will have. Most importantly, a good mentor will want their sidekick to exceed them in skill and knowledge one day. Therefore, it is important to expose them to other superheroes in the field. By exposing the sidekicks to real-world experiences, they can gain valuable training and skill. Introducing your mentee to your contacts, introducing them to other superheroes, and introducing them to experts in the field will help a sidekick begin to build their own networks. This will serve them well as they begin to build their own career. Remember that you are training a sidekick to eventually become a superhero one day. The best way to do this is to help them become connected and exposed in the field of superheroes.

SUPERFRIENDS: ALLIANCES, NETWORKING, & TEAMWORK

"Teamwork is the ability to work together toward a common vision. The ability to direct individual accomplishments toward organizational objectives. It is the fuel that allows common people to attain uncommon results."
Andrew Carnegie

33

Forming Alliances and Assembling a Team: When the Mission is too Big for One Superhero

Many times, superheroes work alone to accomplish missions. Sometimes it's quicker, easier, or more convenient. However, there come times when the problems or missions are too great, too important, or too daunting for any one superhero to accomplish alone. The solo superhero may not have the power of talent alone to deal with the situation. When this occurs, it becomes advantageous to team with other superheroes or form alliances. Sometimes you find that your mission goals align with other superheroes (and sometimes villains), and you all want to accomplish this mission because it is greater than the pride of any one person or superhero. This is when you form an alliance or team to accomplish the mission.

When forming teams or alliances, it becomes very clear that all parties must have the same goal in mind. The mission is very important. Sometimes teams are randomly put together. However, if you are lucky, you can select the members of your team or alliance. If this is the case, then you must choose the right members to be successful. When choosing a team, you must first evaluate your mission or purpose. This mission defines what the team will need to accomplish and what tools you will need. Ideal team members should be able to work with other people, should be versatile, should believe in the mission, and should be dedicated to the mission.

Never doubt that a small group of thoughtful, committed people can change the world. Indeed, it is the only thing that ever has.

~Margaret Meade

34

Leading a Team:
How do you lead a Superhero team?

Sometimes you can choose to be a leader of other superheroes. Other times, leadership can be thrust on you. The leader can be the one to assemble the team or alliances or s/he can be the one chosen to lead the team or alliance once it is assembled. If you find yourself in the position of leadership of an alliance, it is a very important position. The team leader can be the person responsible for facilitating, planning, or developing a strategy, or the team leader can be the point person for making sure the plan is carried out or accomplished.

The team leader is responsible for keeping the members of the team working together for the good of the mission. Leaders must also be willing to dismiss or remove team members who are not contributing or if they are sabotaging efforts of the team to reach their goal. The lead superhero makes sure the alliance accomplishes its mission with minimum injuries, no loss of members, no causalities, no loss of equipment, and no loss of the whole world!

The team leader must evaluate the plan and make changes as needed to protect the team members or to accomplish the mission as new obstacles arise and circumstances change. This leader must know all the aspects of the plan and the role of each of the members so that they can adjust, be able to make substitutions, or be able to step into the void if the need arises. Lastly, the team leader must be willing to take responsibility for any mistake, losses, or shortcomings of the team. While doing so, they mustn't take any credit for any of their team members' success or victories. The team leader places the success of the mission above their position or any recognition or praise. As a team leader, you must:

1) Communicate the mission clearly to all the team members.

2) Evaluate the strengths and abilities of each team member. Often a good way to do this is through one-on-one conversation. By talking with each team member to hear their perspectives on the team, their roles, and/or contributions to the team, the team leader can gather valuable information. This is achieved simply through listening to their understanding of the mission and what they perceive to be the best way to achieve it.

3) Define the roles of the team members so that everyone knows what they are responsible for and expected to do. The team leader is responsible for making sure that each member of the team/alliance knows their role and can carry out that part.

4) Formulate and outline the plan of action for achieving the mission. Be open to teammate criticism and ideas.

Recap: How to Lead a Superhero Team

1. Communicate the mission clearly.
2. Evaluate the strengths and abilities of each team member.
3. Define the roles of the team members.
4. Formulate and outline the plan of action.

"You put together the best team that you can with the players you've got, and replace those who aren't good enough."
Robert Crandal

35
The Superhero Mission

Superheroes that stand the test of time, the test of change, the test of battle, and the test of chaos do not just haphazardly perform their jobs and duty. These superheroes take all their talents and skills and focus them towards a guided goal. This guided goal is the superhero's mission. That mission is the defining element of a superhero's career and legacy. Contained in this chapter are the stages, components, and methodologies needed for carrying out a successful mission.

"Not everything faced can be changed, but nothing can be changed until it is faced."
James Baldwin

Choosing a Mission:
How do you find your calling?

Every superhero must have a mission, cause, purpose, or focus. Sometimes the mission is chosen by the superhero. Other times the mission chooses the superhero. Every mission has its base or beginning where a need must be fulfilled. In society, there are many needs that must be satisfied, and each of these needs is a mission waiting to be accepted. A superhero must have a mission. Some of us will have one mission because the need is so large and very involved. Others will have many smaller missions because they can handle them.

Missions can be defined and limited by geographic location, while other missions can be found in causes that have no geographic boundary. There are some superheroes who choose missions that may be national or international in their scope. On the other hand, some missions can immediate and affect those in the superheroes' local vicinity. Then, there are superheroes that choose missions which are international, national, and local in scope. To complete missions, many superheroes unite and connect with other superheroes to tackle larger missions. Superheroes with the same type of assignment often collaborate with each other. Yet, there are those superheroes who tackle their mission alone.

It is very important that a superhero carefully chooses which missions to accept because they are defined by their missions. The mission is how a superhero does good deeds in the world. It's not by completing random acts of good alone, but by using their extraordinary abilities to fulfill the needs that

are unmet in the world. A superhero stands in and fills the
gaps that those unfulfilled needs create.

36
The Superhero Method:
Think like a Superhero

Rules and processes are part of all successful occupations, businesses, or careers. Like in any other successful occupation, there is a method or process to being a good superhero or to "proper superhero-ing." Successful superheroes follow this method whether intentionally or by forced mistakes. Although the method will vary from superhero to superhero, it may gain some details and steps (or lose some). Regardless, it is basically the same process. The superhero method is how a superhero carries out their work and fulfills their mission.

"A winner is someone who recognizes his God-given talents, works his tail off to develop them into skills and uses these skills to accomplish his goals."
Larry Bird

37
Jumping into Action

When a situation arises or a problem occurs, the superhero springs into action, but not before they formulate a plan (...unless they're a rookie.) Most times, superheroes can process things very quickly (experienced heroes can process even faster). Therefore, it may not seem that they pause to think at all. However, in the pause or moment between inaction and action in the superhero's mind, a plan formulates. It is at this moment that the superhero takes time to S.E.E. the situation: Survey, Evaluate, and Execute.

SURVEY. The first thing that the hero does is to Survey the scene. What is going on? What problem is occurring? In surveying the scene, the hero can see what is the immediate problem, what is the initial cause of the problem, what are the immediate dangers, and what needs immediate attention. Surveying also allows a superhero to see what resources or tools are around that can be used, are being used, or need to be used. Surveying allows a superhero to understand the atmosphere and environment before they enter and expose themselves or others to danger. In addition to resources and tools, surveying will let a superhero identify people who can help or people who will hinder the process.

EVALUATE. The second step is to Evaluate. In this step, a superhero must evaluate the situation in terms of the measure of response that will be needed. Is the situation a minor problem or is it a level ten, five-alarm, or "def con" emergency? This allows the superhero to determine what amount of resources is needed and the speed and amount which must be applied. In evaluating the situation, you can determine the proper response level.

As a superhero begins to evaluate, they add up the cost of the response needed versus the damage caused by the problem or situation. Critical problems may require substantial resources and may have a high cost in terms of energy, effort, time, and equipment. In the Evaluate step, you begin to formulate a plan which has a balance between the cost, benefits, risks, and the desired goal. The superhero in this step also weighs the urgency of time in this situation. Is a rapid response, slower tempo, or longer pace strategy needed for the situation? Note that it helps when a superhero has good awareness or knowledge of their talents and skills in advance.

EXECUTE. The final step is to Execute the plan. This is the most important step because it is the follow through with the action. A superhero must put the plan in motion. Remember that no plan will go perfectly as planned, but one-hundred percent of the plans never tried or attempted fail one-hundred percent of the time. Once you have surveyed and evaluated, execute the best plan as possible. If that does not work and if the problem is not solved, then repeat the process. Regrouping and re-evaluating are viable steps to correcting your course of action. Keep reevaluating and keep up your efforts. Based on the experience level of the superhero, these steps could occur in a blink of an eye, or it could take longer. When a superhero gets really good, you won't notice the pause of the steps at all. But, trust they are always there.

"A goal without a plan is just a wish".
- Antoine de Saint Exupery

ACHIEVING SUPERHERO STATUS

"Great ability develops and reveals itself increasingly with every new assignment."
Baltasar Gracian

38
The Ultimate Level

The Ultimate level is about the drive to be the best. All superheroes have a desire to achieve or reach the ultimate level by becoming the elite of superheroes, the premiere, the best, and the ultimate. The quest to achieve the level of the elite and exclusive requires superheroes to achieve skill and status reserved for the few. All superheroes strive to be better, to do better, and to be the best at what they do. It is an ingrained desired in the mind and work ethic of every superhero.

Superheroes are competitive with each other, with rivals, and with themselves. Out of the competition comes a drive that pushes the superhero to excel. These leaders have various skill levels and levels of experience. It is their experiences, adventures, missions, victories, and even defeats which push a superhero towards the ultimate level. No matter what level a superhero starts, the drive of the superhero pushes them to get better and to rise higher and higher.

39
Sidekick Status

Sidekick status is the beginning level for superheroes in the making who show great potential and talent. Hopefully, the talent is recognized by an established superhero who takes them under their wing to give them some directions, mentoring, and training. A sidekick works behind the scenes learning, watching, gaining experience, and seeking opportunities to use their powers. Eager and enthusiastic, a sidekick is self-motivated to get better, to learn, and to grow. Sidekick status is born out of the desire to help people, to influence people, to help the community, and to change the world. The time spent at the sidekick level depends on several factors: their mentor, their skill level, and their desire.

Champion Status

Champion status is achieved when a difficult mission is completed. Champions are crowned after a great victory or accomplishment. This leader has proven to be the best on that particular day, particular season, or that particular skill area. The champion can become very popular and enjoy great accolades from this one great mission or good accomplishment. They can be remembered for that one act or mission. A champion can be trapped as a victor unless they try more difficult missions or tasks and fail.

For a champion to progress to the next level, they have to take a chance. By attempting harder missions and more difficult tasks, the champion takes a great chance of failure and making mistakes. For a victor, losses and public mistakes can cause them to lose favor and popularity. For some people, being a champion is good enough. The risk of trying harder things and risking losing popularity and status is not worth it to them. Achieving a great mission is difficult enough to do once and even more difficult to do twice. They find that they can live off the status and fame of their one great victory. However, the memory of that victory only lives for so long.

Superhero Status

Superhero status is when superheroes do work and make an impact. This status level is reserved for those who have managed a consistently high work level with a high output level. A superhero status leader consistently accepts and achieves missions of high difficulty and high complexity which have broad impacts. They accept the missions others do not want or do not have the skill to accomplish them. Their powers and skills have evolved to a level of consistent high output and focus. They have a steady vision and work to make their visions happen. Most importantly, at this status level, leaders choose and accept missions because there is a need. A superhero of this status inspires confidence in those around them by consistently pushing themselves to achieve and do better. They lead by example and make others around them better as well.

This status is difficult to achieve and harder to maintain. Superheroes are often celebrated in some circles but simultaneously criticized in others. However, they complete their missions amid criticisms and conflicts. They believe in their missions strongly enough to continue them regardless of popularity, help, accolades, or rewards. For a superhero to progress to the final and ultimate level, time and longevity are needed.

Legend Status

Legend status is only populated by a few superheroes. Only the elite of the elite can ever hope to reach this level. Although there are exceptions, legend status is rarely awarded or achieved while a superhero is on active duty or during their career. The influence of superheroes at this stage is felt by generations. These superhero legends' deeds are known far and wide, and their adventures are told and retold. The faults and shortcomings of the superhero may have faded from memory, but the results of their good deeds have been magnified. Their career was such or they accomplished a mission so great that they are elevated to legend status because everyone is in awe of their accomplishment. The legends accomplished things that no one else could accomplish in the face of odds that no one else could overcome.

The method and style of a legend superhero become the roadmap and the model for other superheroes to follow, to study, to aspire, and to duplicate. Their thought process and tendency become philosophy for action and problem-solving. Their missions and mission logs become case studies and practice scenarios. Their style is emulated by superheroes, heroes, champions, sidekicks, and everyone else. Legend superheroes become the inspiration, the motivation, and the model for generations to come.

40

Evolution:
Getting better and moving to the Next Level

Every hero has limits to their abilities. However, every superhero can get better at using their ability, strengthening their existing ability, and sometimes discovering new abilities. The more a superhero uses their abilities and talents, the more comfortable they become with using the ability. In turn, they will feel more comfortable to push themselves to give maximum effort. And, the more they push closer to their limit and push their limit, the greater the chance that their powers will evolve. Evolution is when a superhero surpasses their preconceived limit of their abilities, discovers a new hidden ability, or finds a greater depth to their power. It takes a superhero to a different power level.

Growth only occurs when a superhero pushes themselves to get better. One of the best ways this can happen is by training. Training allows a superhero to practice their abilities and learn about them before a big battle. It allows a superhero to become comfortable with their powers and assess their limits. Sometimes training can take place in private or by accepting smaller missions or tasks. These smaller missions or tasks can be chosen to focus on using a different or specific ability or to become familiar with a scenario or mission parameters.

Training can also require the leader to better understand their abilities through study. A superhero may read about different battle techniques and updated battle strategies, study film of previous battles, or study the work of an expert superhero in the same field or with the same type of mission. Knowledge is a very powerful tool for any hero to push the limit of their ability.

A superhero sometimes evolves by partnering with other superheroes more experienced or more powerful than them. The more powerful and experienced superhero pushes them to get better and raises their skill level which causes them to evolve. Other times the superhero evolves by gradually taking on missions which are harder, more difficult, and more involved. A superhero cannot be concerned with failing or small losses because often the experience is valuable knowledge needed to get stronger, to get better, and to evolve to the next level.

There are times when defeat by a superior opponent can spur and inspire a superhero to evolve and to get better. A superior opponent can push you past your limits and cause you to evolve to keep up. If you stay at the same power level for your whole career or never accept missions that are more of a challenge, you are wasting all your talents and potential because you will never grow or evolve.

"Character cannot be developed in ease and quiet. Only through experiences of trial and suffering can the soul be strengthened, vision cleared, ambition inspired and success achieved."
Helen Keller

THE ULTIMATE TEST
and
MEASURE

"Far better it is to dare mighty things, to win glorious triumphs even though checkered by failure, than to rank with those poor spirits who neither enjoy nor suffer much because they live in the gray twilight that knows neither victory nor defeat."
Theodore Roosevelt.

41

The Never-ending Battle

The work hours of a superhero can be long. Although there are breaks between missions and adventures, the battle is continuous. The never-ending battle means that a superhero will always be engaged in a battle if they are an active superhero. There are innumerous missions and needs in the world that need fulfilling. In the scope of those missions, there are people who need help, villains who must be fought, and ideas that must be protected. The world will always need superheroes.

There is never a time when a superhero can say that they're done with every task and mission and there is nothing more for them to do. A superhero may accomplish or complete a mission in one area, clean up one area, or make one community safe, but there are always places that need their help. Consequently, sometimes superheroes move as they are needed. The battles are "never-ending" because there is always work to be done.

If you find yourself bored with nothing to do, you are either not looking hard enough, not living up to your potential, or you're fighting battles in the wrong arena. Sometimes as the battle count rises, it can be easy to lose focus of your mission or objective. Therefore, you must keep revisiting your mission and making sure you are staying the course. Superheroes can get tired but must keep going; that's why they are superheroes. They are meant to do the things other people cannot, will not, or are not able to do.

Just as a superhero is not defined by wearing a cape, leaders are not defined by championships, titles, rings, trophies, or belts. Instead, they are defined by their hearts. Their willingness to fight on when everyone else has quit, grace in defeat, and knowing that winning is not the only thing are at the core of the heart of every superhero. Moreover, a superhero is defined by their journey, the paths they choose to walk, the loyalty they show the people who walk beside them, and the joy of the people who choose to follow them.

Most importantly, a superhero is defined by the hope that they give to others. It is that hope which unites those who would be divided by giving them a common cause to believe in, a common sense of purpose, and a common identity. A true superhero - through their journey, through their battles, through their fights, and through their defeats - inspires and encourages the hearts and minds of countless others. Long after titles have been forgotten, trophies and medals have faded, and records have been broken, the impact of true leadership lives on. Because inspiration by leadership does not reside on a shelf or in a glass case, it rests in the heart and minds of those who would be superheroes, and its impact is infinite.

The Superhero Survey

Are you ready to begin your superhero journey? Are you ready to increase your leadership skills? Use the Superhero Status Survey below to begin.

1. Can you recognize a superhero when you see one in action?
2. Can you identify the superhero talents within yourself and others?
3. Do you know what it takes to be a superhero and achieve superhero status?
4. Can you identify your superhero style?
5. Can you recognize the superhero style of other superheroes?
6. Can you think of other superhero profiles?
7. Can you identify your own superpowers?
8. Can you recognize other potential superpowers that you can acquire?
9. Can you recognize the superpowers possessed by others?
10. Can you recognize the superhero lessons which pertain to your current situation?
11. Can you recognize how the Superhero lessons can help you with a situation?
12. Can you recognize when you see the Superhero lessons being put into action?
13. Can you think of other superhero lessons that you need to learn?
14. Can you identify a villain when you encounter them?

15. Can you recognize the traits, strengths, and weaknesses of the villains you encounter?
16. Can you think of other potential villain profiles?
17. Can you recognize the Villain lessons which pertain to your current situation?
18. Can you recognize how the Villain lessons can help you achieve your mission?
19. Can you recognize when you see the Villain lessons being put into action?
20. Can you recognize what it will take for you to become a superhero?
21. Can you recognize which superhero mentor is best for you?
22. Can recognize skills you need to learn to become a full-fledged superhero?
23. Can you recognize the superhero potential in others?
24. Can you share your knowledge and wisdom with others?
25. Are you willing to help potential superheroes to grow?
26. Can you recognize when a situation requires assembling a team?
27. Can you recognize what type of team members are needed for a strong team?
28. Can you make a mission purpose clear for a team of superheroes to follow?
29. Do you know how to work with other superheroes?
30. Do you know how to balance your powers with those of your team or alliance?
31. Do you know how to pick your mission?
32. Can you recognize how the Superhero mission shapes the career of the superhero?

33. Can recognize what it will take to accomplish your mission?
34. Can you S.E.E. how to win in any situation?
35. What is your current superhero level?
36. At what superhero level do you aspire to be?
37. How do you plan to achieve your desired superhero level?
38. What is the ultimate measure of a superhero?
39. How do you measure up to the superhero standard?
40. How will you be ultimately measured as a superhero?
41. How will you be tested as a superhero?
42. In what ways have you already been tested?
43. How will you pass the tests of a superhero?
44. What will your superhero origin story begin?
45. Are you ready to become a superhero?

About the Author

Dr. Ashley B. Hosey is an author, speaker, and educator. He received his BFA degree from the University of Georgia in Athens, his M.ED from the State University of West Georgia and his Ed.D from the University of Alabama.

In his 20 plus years as an educator he has worked in both the high school and elementary levels in addition to working in an alternative school setting. He has served both urban, suburban, rural and at risk populations. Dr. Hosey has worked with countless student, youth groups and mentor groups throughout his career.

He is a husband to his beautiful wife and the proud father to two wonderful children. His hope is that his writing and thoughts will motivate and inspire others to use their talents, find their confidence and to make a difference in the lives of others.

Additional Acknowledgements
Dr. Hosey would like to thank all those who helped him, encouraged him and supported him on this project: His wife, family, friends, the Crue, the Johnson Tribe Publishing group, Val Pugh Love Editing, August Pride, Garnett Publishing, his current students and former students.

To Contact Dr. Hosey:
By Mail:
Garnett Publishing
P.O. Box 1311
Powders Springs, Ga 30127
Email: abhosey@drhoseyleads.com
Website/Blog: www.drhoseyleads.com